A concise and highly
reach specific goals.

"Anyone feeling stuck careers, or in a transition of in Sharon Hooper's new book, *From Dreams to Action: A Proven Method to Achieve Your Goals*. Words of sage advice offer not only practicality and a strategic approach to achieve your goals, but they also provide a creative approach. Hooper's unique Vision Mapping Strategies concept is both brilliant and helpful. Should you be motivated to achieve greater success, you are encouraged to read this book today, as it is written to put you on the direct path for getting to your goal more effectively."

—Elinor Stutz, "Top 1% Social Marketing Influencer, by the Marketing Hub."
Author of bestselling *Nice Girls Do Get the Sale* and *The Wish*

"Sharon is masterful at helping us reveal our dreams, life goals and next strategies to ourselves. She pulls out, catalyzes and makes real all those loose thread of thoughts and swirling ideas into a tapestry of action and new possibility...all in a remarkably short period of time. Vision Mapping and coaching with Sharon is one of the smartest moves anyone can make who is serious about actualizing their vision."

—Wib Middleton Co-owner, Thunder Mountain Design & Communications
www.ThunderMountainDesign.com

"Sharon has been my coach since 1999...she has coached me professionally and personally, helping me to make tough decisions which helped my business grow. I did vision mapping with her in person and on the phone. She is an awesome individual with high integrity and patience, and I have known her for over 15 years. Her teaching style is firm and friendly. You will enjoy working with her and she can help you accomplish anything you wish for."

—Juuhi Ahuja, President & CEO, Wise Men Group, Houston, Texas

Vision Mapping Strategies with Sharon is a MUST! If you are interested in growing your income, growing your business, and having more freedom to do what you truly want...Sharon shows you how. For your success and fulfillment in life and business, I highly recommend her."

—Dr. Gayle, Psychologist, CO

"Throughout our process with Vision Mapping Strategies, Sharon helped us clarify our visions for our future. She provided information about tools, resources and strategies we had not been aware of. Of equal important to understanding the big picture, we came away with very specific action steps to take over the next 4 – 6 weeks, planting us more firmly on our path and accelerating our progress. Sharon utilizes life coaching skills and draws on her formidable business background to create an opportunity for Inspiration to flow through us all. We highly recommend Sharon's work for those who are ready to move successfully into the future.

—Eric and Linda Haggard, Sedona Integrative Medical Clinic

"I have had several vision mapping sessions with Ms. Hooper and I am so happy to see that she has now published her foolproof method and made it available to all who are seeking support through their life transits. Ms. Hooper's work has helped to support me in finding my career niche after my child left home, for example, through guiding me to find within what I really want and need to do in this lifetime. I can't recommend this book more."

—Deborah L. Neff, Ph.D.

This breakthrough book shows how to use Sharon Hooper's powerful Vision Mapping technique on your own to organize all your creative ideas, thoughts and desires into doable action steps that will lead you on an empowering, practical path to success. Her technique is an amazing organizing tool that channels all your energy in a focused direction so you can easily plan day by day, week by week, and month by month, exactly what you need to be doing to reach your goals... whether it's a business or a personal goal. When Sharon first introduced Vision Mapping to me it was a huge "Aha" moment for me, and I've been using it ever since. Her private clients pay her well to access this tool, and in this book you'll learn exactly how to use it yourself without the expense of hiring her as your coach. (Although she still takes on some clients and does seminars on it too.)

If you have an inkling about something you'd like to do, but aren't sure how you'll get there, or feel overwhelmed by the amount of work it might take to succeed, this is a great book for you. As the title says, "From Dreams to Action," this is exactly what this book does, and if you read it and follow the advice, you'll see yourself moving ahead toward your goals in a way you may not have thought was possible. Go for it!

—J. G. Frank, author of *House Selling Blues* and *Things to do in Portland* OR

"Sharon is gifted with so many talents. Experiencing her passion and joy while vision mapping together has awakened my creative side. Her laser focus insights and coaching have inspired me to put the pieces together into a solid action plan. Within a few minutes, she offered me an outline to play with to bring my book into creation now! I love Sharon's no nonsense action approach, infused with lots of love and support. If you have a dream and are ready to make it reality but are not sure where to start or find yourself procrastinating, then do yourself a favor and contact Sharon. Joyful blessings."

—Tina van Leuven, Ph.D, www.innerdelight.com

"The next best thing to personally working one on one with Sharon Hooper is following Sharon's step by step action plan in "From Dreams to Action." Your deepest dreams can be realized if you can get them out of your head. I found this to be so true. My dream became more real once I was empowered to move in the world of action one carefully thought out step a a time. Sharon's ability to identify what was needed at each crossroad is what sets her apart from other coaches and authors. She taught me how to dig deep to find what will nourish not just my bank account but my soul."

—C. Cohn, Seattle, WA.

"Sharon's unique combination of business acumen, intuitive and visionary skills will bring the focus and clarity required in the pursuit of your destiny and dreams. Her vision mapping process showed me the way to plan and strategize my goals. She possesses an unwavering commitment to her clients; she will bestow upon you her limitless gifts thus insuring your success. She's a no nonsense person when it comes to her dedication and tenacity; she will never allow you to give up as quitting just is not her style".

—Roz Reynolds, Psychic, AZ

"I want to express my gratitude to you for all your unbelievable help in bringing about the vision of my business from a wee thought to a focused and strategic plan. With your vision mapping strategies journey, not only was this process great fun, but a creative, results-oriented blue print for what I need to be doing NOW. I have my vision map taped up on the wall of my office where I can see the direction I am heading every day. Your continued coaching is opening up even more exciting possibilities as I continue this process of reaching my goals. Thank you for helping me to express what I want to create for my business and for myself."

—Richard Lynch, President, Sedona Adventures & Tours

"Thank you for the incredible business coaching and strategies session! The vision mapping is a dynamic process that was instrumental in helping me organize my goals, create a plan of action and inspire new possibility's...Your incredible facilitation helped me shift my dream into a huge YES!"

—Belle Shook, Equine Therapist, AZ

"Sharon, Being in your Vision Mapping class series has been like having my own personal coach. I have been challenged, strengthened, enlightened and supported. Your Vision Mapping process is creative and exciting and fun to work through with the group. My goals developed authentically from my connection to self and to Spirit, facilitated by your coaching. I've been amazed that I am meeting all of my goals in a way that I would not have otherwise realized. I can tell that you really immerse yourself in this work that you love and it shows. Thank you so much!"

—Andrea Beaudoin, www.alignyourenergy.com

"Sharon Hooper combines gentleness and keen insight and clear direction in her vision journeys work–a rare mix which makes it all the more powerful and inspiring."

—Dr. Stephen M. Marcus, founder www.mbono.net

Sharon Hooper's Vision Mapping is a journey everyone should experience. It helped me uncover my true desires and intentions for the future, allowed me to focus on how to make a difference in my personal and professional life, and gave me a strategic plan of action that is not only achievable but energizing. Sharon is the ultimate guide in your quest for "True North"!

—Michele Miller, Phoenix

Sharon's Vision Mapping Course was awesome! Her energy, enthusiasm and expertise in guiding me through my life's vision was enlightening and incredibly fun at the same time. I really enjoyed the interactive style of her classes and came away from the course full of inspiration, motivation and clarity on how to move forward with my dreams. This was one of the best things I have ever done for myself. I highly recommend working with Sharon."

—Jean Drummond, L.Ac. Acupuncturist/Health & Wellness Consultant • www.thewellnesspotential.com

FROM DREAMS TO ACTION

A PROVEN METHOD TO ACHIEVE YOUR GOALS

Sharon L. Hooper
www.SharonHooper.com

From Dreams to Action:
A Proven Method to Achieve Your Goals

Copyright ©2018 by Sharon L. Hooper
All rights reserved

Perfect Bound First Edition

Publishing services by W. Bruce Conway
Cover art by www.ThunderMountainDesign.com
Sedona, Arizona

All rights reserved. No part of this publication may be reproduced, stored in a retrieval system or transmitted, in any form or by any means without the prior written permission of the author, nor be otherwise circulated in any form of binding or cover other than that in which it is published and without a similar condition being imposed on the purchaser.

ISBN 978-1-9843-8350-1

www.SharonHooper.com

Printed and distributed by CreateSpace,
an Amazon.com company

Dedication

To all you passionate journeyers
who are mapping the life
of your dreams and goals.

Contents

Introduction: Visioning: strong and clear… how it leads to success - 1

Lesson One: Preparing the Groundwork for Your Action Plan - 13

Lesson Two: Bringing Increased Awareness to the Vision Mapping Strategies Process - 22

Lesson Three: Digging Deeper into Who You Are in Preparation for Your Action Plan - 33

Lesson Four: Creating the Actual Vision Map – First Steps - 43

Lesson Five: Action is the Key to Success - 53

Lesson Six: Carrying Out Your Action Plan - 64

Afterword: Review and Coordination of Vision/Goal Implementation - 68

Books and Resources: For Further Exploration & Discovery - 71

Introduction

How many times have you started something, only to lose focus or interest long before your idea has come to life?

You have all had successes. And probably, you have tried something and then lost steam.

What do you recall about those successes? If you were to jot them down and look at the list for a few minutes, would you observe any particular themes about how and why you were successful?

This same exercise holds true for projects that lost energy for you. Listing these 'almost-made-it-happen' ideas, are their underlying actions that prevented you from reaching your desired outcome?

Taking the time to process a few of these past experiences will create insights as you craft your perfect goal and then follow that with your exciting and achievable plan of action. The instructions in this book will give you a specific method to design the plans for your next success.

Strong and clear goals + commitment + action = Success

Through my own experiences with non-successes, I realized that there were many people who had a pattern of: start / stop / pick up where I left off / become unmotivated / start again when inspired / quit the project and file it in a drawer. I know some of you are smiling right now because you have been in a similar circumstance… maybe more than once.

Often, I began projects with excitement and a vision for the completed goal, but occasionally, somewhere along the way, I got derailed by some life event, or lost interest because my brilliant idea was taking too long to shape up. When, in *my* mind, the project finally seemed doomed, I would feel defeated – and hesitant to start another one because I had failed – *again*! And believe me, there have been a few *not-so-successes* in my past.

Two of my greatest successes were co-creating an independent record label and forging a model child care center for more than 300 children daily.

The record label was introduced into the gift industry, and resulted in multi-million dollar sales annually, in less than five years. Laughing now, I remember the gift trade consultant telling Richard (my husband) and me that we had a 'cute idea,' but that we would never make more than $60,000 a year in the gift industry.

Yet there we were, millions of dollars later. Well, that's definitely a surprising story of its own. **Lesson learned**: Of course, reality is important and must be taken seriously. But remember that faith in your abilities and your own gut feelings are as important as all the 'facts' you discover when you are planning your new venture.

Some of our CD covers

Before the record label venture, the U.S. Army at Ft. Ord, California, was searching for a new Child Care Center Director to manage a facility that cared for 300 children, every day, from the ages of six weeks to ten years. I was hired for the job. All I can say is that I have never, to date, experienced any job as fulfilling, and stressful, and one that offered me the freedom to create an environment where everyone flourished, including the caregivers.

More recently I produced **The Wisdom of Mary Magdalene** inspirational card deck, and a spicy 1870's Victorian novella filled with unique and memorable characters. These tasks were achieved with clarity, focus and persistence.

Many young companies reach the cusp of turning the corner from weakness to achievement when the entrepreneur abandons hope because the business is seen as failing – when ironically, success is literally just one more step away.

Best practices have shown that anyone can manifest a goal or dream *if* they use a very simple formula, and *if* they are truly passionate about their topic.

Vision + Action + Perseverance = Success

Knowing what it takes to bring a vision forth is different than having **the drive to make something specific happen.** At times, it was challenging to even figure out my own goals, unsure about the best direction to take because I couldn't get focused on the next leg of my journey. My own thoughts (and those of my friends) contributed so much chatter about what I should do that I often felt thoroughly confused and just gave up the dream pursuit.

This is where the thought of **Vision Mapping** became a continual thought in my head, and then became a reality in my work as a Life and Business Coach.

Vision mapping is the distillation of abstract ideas that transition into the world of specific actions.

Over the years I've attended many workshops which brought me right to the edge of exploration and clarity, but all the creativity and discovery didn't provide me with a real method to move forward with my idea. Where was the strategic plan of action? As an experienced business woman, consultant, and Professional Certified Coach, I kept playing with the vision of helping people become **clear and focused**. I wanted to show people how to create their own process that would lead them to a successful conclusion.

This program, **Vision Mapping Strategies** ©, is a complete process that takes individuals and groups from their vision through a strategic plan of action to the successful achievement of their goal. With it, I want to help you short circuit confusion and get as centered as possible so that you can gain clarity about your actual choice of goals.

Following the processes in this course will assist you in creating your own personal and strategic action plan. Maintain focus, stay committed and take as much time as you need.

Goal + Insight + Committed Action = Accomplishment

In 2003 (after coaching formally for three years) I came to the realization that many of us get stuck in the "How do I make this happen?" stage – not with the idea or the vision – but by the lack of an actual step by step system that can guide us to our desired result. Visions and goals often get stuck. Multitudes of thoughts may be going through our minds, and it can be challenging to know what comes first and how to tease apart all the pieces to make *it* a reality. Believe in your own strong abilities and with the support of this Course, you can shape your passion into a strong plan of action…piece by piece.

How* are you going to define what you want and *how* you are going to get there?

That's what Vision Mapping is all about: gaining clarity, focus and constructing a blueprint to arrive at your desired destination.

Until now, the process of *Vision Mapping Strategies* has been facilitated by me through Skype or in person. However, I am continually asked for a self-paced program that can be used at home. This Course can be the perfect option for you.

Set your own pace for completing each of the six Lessons — but do be sure to work through them in sequence. Each section is designed to move you from one step to the next. Laying down the groundwork and committing to your process will help define exactly what you desire to accomplish before you start constructing your actual Vision Map, which is the heart of your plan.

When I think about manifesting a vision, my philosophy is to go to the edge of my [your] comfort zone. That's where the potential for real growth is present, regardless of the topic. This edge creates a new (and larger) footprint for you to grow into. When you begin forming these new imprints, you'll realize how much you have grown since the previous step, and you will be motivated to take yet another quantum leap into what might be unknown territory.

This Course is intended to share ideas and the specific

method I employ which has guided hundreds of people to their own success. However, this is your dream and you can materialize it in any way you choose. I look forward to hearing from you about your "aha's," your successes, your stumbling blocks, and any eureka moments you wish to share.

Even if you are not sure of what your vision might be, this Course will provide many ideas for possibilities. Always focus on the things you want, rather than the things you don't want.

A positive motto can be: 'do something – don't stand still'. The answers will come with bold exploration.

If you are serious about embracing your goal, each Lesson will require some quiet time on your part. That means no email, no cell phone, no company – just you and your intelligence, intuition, creativity and visions. Create a safe space for your vision to flourish – for instance, a special nook in your house, or outdoors, where your mind is free from distractions and you can concentrate on your journey… a surrounding that will inspire you to dig deeper, to gain increased clarity as you start to plan your strategies.

Set aside forty-five minutes to an hour so that you can thoughtfully consider the reflection questions. Think of this Course as your own private retreat which can be accomplished in the privacy of your home, by the ocean, on a mountain top. You get to choose the location that inspires you to stretch into your vision – the dream you are coaxing into reality.

Clear Vision

"Clear Vision" is a thought picture that you can turn into real action through a conscious and systematic process. **"Visioning"** is a mental picture of your achievement *before* it happens. It supports you in looking inward to discover your own wisdom.

**A compelling vision comes from within, not somewhere outside of you.
It's a tool for self-direction.
Clear vision is your real
expression in the world.**

All throughout history high achievers have had a common trait: the ability to see their visions in 3D long before actually achieving their goals. They used visualization as a conscious and systematic process to accomplish their hopes and desires. As early as the 6th century, through Tantric yoga, Buddhists used a system of holding images in their minds for the desired outcome. Modern yogis focus their will or attention, and reinforce that focus with affirmations and suggestions.

You may have heard about the study conducted by Harvard Business School for students in the 1979 MBA program. The results prove the validity of the ways clear goals and plans create success. Students were asked: "Have you set clear, written goals for your future and made plans to accomplish them?" Three per cent of these graduates had written goals and plans; thirteen per cent had goals, but not in writing. And eighty-four percent had no goals at all.

When the members of this class were interviewed ten years later in 1989, the results were remarkable. The 13% of students who had goals were earning about twice as much as the 84% who had no goals at all. **But the students who had clear and written goals were earning (on average) ten times as much as the other 97 percent put together!**

Goals don't have to be financially oriented, of course. Most people I have guided through this vision-to-action process seek to improve their income – not just to have more money for its own sake – but because a surplus of money meant having the freedom to do as they wished.

A strong core of self-knowledge, before delving into an explicit and targeted method for your future plans will provide a solid foundation of who you are. The first priority is to identify exactly what you stand for…and then slide gently into specific direction with a discerning focal point. You might even be surprised at your responses to the questions I'll be asking you during the Vision Mapping process – answers that can alter your course of action.

If you can put a name to what you are looking for, your path will feel more solid as you explore your true calling.

Sometimes you may ask,

"How will I even know when I've found what I'm searching for?"

Ahhh... this is an age-old question.

When you transition from yearning for something, to the peacefulness of being fully present in each moment, you have reached the essence of your own truth and fulfillment.

**Materials you will need to create
your Vision Map:**

> Markers in your favorite colors (at least four or five different colors)

> A pad of non-lined easel paper (for Lessons 4 through 6, can be purchased at any office store)

> Pen/pencil (you'll use these after you finish your Vision Mapping process)

Lesson One

Preparing the Groundwork for Your Action Plan

The first three Lessons are designed to help you get into the flow of *who* you are, which will provide clarity when you begin your actual Vision Map (which you will begin in Lesson Four). While processing these first Lessons, you will get an overview of why Vision Mapping your own blueprint for success is so valuable.

Committing daily to do *something* towards your goal will bring you closer and closer to the result you desire. If you have questions as this Course progresses, write them down and think them through. The answers will probably emerge as you process further. However, if you feel stuck at any time, email me (Sharon@VisionJourneys.com) and we can talk about private coaching via phone or Skype.

Sometimes we get stuck in the "how" of making something happen.

Your Vision Map is a blueprint for action, showing you tangibly HOW to bring your dreams and vision into the world.

Move forward with your own style of compassionate action through the service that you provide to others.

Mapping your visions into a cohesive strategy will move you forward with an achievable and passionate plan of action geared to your unique needs and the specific results you desire. Others may be impatient for you to reach your goals. Remember that this is *your* life, *your* goal – not someone else's dream. *your dreams*

Now that you are beginning to understand how valuable your Vision Map will be for reaching the goal you desire, it's time to think about your *pre-Vision Mapping foundation*. The exercises for this first Lesson involve warm-ups to help you stretch your mind in the pursuit of converting ideas to actual strategies for the results you desire.

To start gaining focus about why you are seeking clarity on a topic or goal, you will be asked to answer *reflection* questions. I strongly advise you to take plenty of time and to write down your responses. This is an opportune exercise for centering yourself.

Visualization + clarity + focus + desire + strong plan of action = success and abundance

Getting Ready to Go Deep

Creating a ritual, or a quiet space before you begin your day's vision work, allows for a peaceful transition where your ideas can flow more smoothly. Most of the time, I prefer spending fifteen minutes in mindfulness meditation. However, the most important idea here is to quiet down the chatter in your head so that your frame of mind can evolve into a visionary one. If you wish to use words in your meditation, this is an example of how to quiet your mind.

> *I close my eyes and picture myself already living my desired goal – experiencing the vibrations of what it feels, sounds, smells and looks like.*
>
> *I notice any doubts or fears that arise and simply note that they are there as I return to the vision of my completed dream and the joy I experience while I am living it.*
>
> *Old negative beliefs are no longer valid, and I am now taking positive action. Now is the time for me to be courageous, to step forward and make my plan, to take it in any direction I choose. If I can dream it, I can achieve it! My idea has gained momentum. I am ready, willing and motivated to give this vision the attention it deserves. This dream is already happening, for I am now giving it form and substance.*

Step into the miracle of YOU and let spirit guide you to fulfillment.

Aligning Your Goals with Your Values

One of the stumbling blocks that people often face is trying to align a goal with their purest values. For instance, my top value is family. I am always there to support and love them, and they are there for me. Another important part of my life is community. I love all the advancements that personal development has given me, and I am passionate about sharing, learning, and teaching others. If my vision didn't allow me to include these beliefs, I would undoubtedly be unsuccessful in reaching my goal, and I would feel as though there was always something missing which prevented my total satisfaction.

Resolve to be a goal-seeking being, moving unerringly toward the things that are important to you.

During a coaching session I asked a former client, Stephen, about the most important value in his life. He responded, "Spending time with family." His dilemma concerned being offered a big promotion that would take him on the road even more than his present job. He didn't know what to do: make more money that was needed for medical purposes and be away from family more hours each week… OR stay with his present job where he was able to spend every weekend and most evenings with his wife and children.

When Stephen understood the importance of his own values, the decision was easy. He never regretted turning down the promotion, even though many colleagues just didn't get it. Stephen was being true to himself, and acting on his own truths which provided him with abundant happiness.

Perhaps your values may involve teaching, traveling, being a spiritual mentor, creating greater income, being of service, playing music, being an entrepreneurial warrior. Write down what is most important to you, items that drive your life every day, values that are essential to you in order to live fully and enjoyably.

Now that you've taken the time to contemplate what's

truly important to you – the values you hold dear and the ethics that hold your life together – you'll want to ensure their inclusion in every aspect of your evolving plan of action… because if your own innate needs are not met, you'll be forever compromising yourself by not including personal ideals along with the game plan for your vision.

Review of Lesson One

This Lesson has been the prelude to a possible reawakening of ambitions and challenges that you weren't ready for – until now. Clients frequently ask me questions like, "Why didn't I leave him/her before?" or "Why have I waited so long to change professions/jobs?" My answer is always that:

We simply do what we need to do until we don't need to do it any more.

It's really that simple – and that complex – simultaneously. We are not ready to take another leg on our life's journey until we come to completion in our hearts and minds with the present situation. We will know when it's time for the next thing. So be gentle with yourself as you move through these Lessons.

There is no need to hurry. You can take six months or even a year if you wish. Remember, however, that there is a difference between procrastination and conscious and deliberate consideration. My only recommendation is that you reach into your heart and mind to answer the questions truthfully. And if necessary, contemplate certain thoughts as long as you need to before moving on.

When we short circuit any aspect of our lives, it's guaranteed that we'll return to the same situation repeatedly until we've dealt with it.

Now that you have some background on how Vision Mapping Strategies work and what the process can do for you, it's time to ask yourself questions about who you are, what you want, what is important to you, and where your passion lies. Having a journal or notebook to hold all your thoughts in one place will be very helpful as you proceed through the lessons.

LESSON ONE
EXERCISE I

Powerful focus is essential in preparing your ultimate strategy. It is so easy for our minds to waste precious time worrying about things that will probably never happen.

Before you delve into this Course, write your vision – your dream for the future – as if it's already accomplished. We'll return to this original vision as the Course continues. There are no limits to this vision (people, money, time, resources) there is only the dream that you hold dear in your heart and head. Write whatever comes to mind. Details are not important here. Write as though you were describing it to your best friend who loves and supports you, knowing that your vision is perfect for you.

LESSON ONE

_____

_____

_____

_____

_____

EXERCISE 2

Why did I purchase this Course? What did I expect to achieve?

What would motivate me to complete this Course in order to realize my vision?

What has stopped me from living my dream in the past?

How is my vision different (or better) than anyone else's dream?

Am I willing to forego some activities in order to put more concentrated time into reaching my goal?

What does "success" mean to me?

How will I know when I've reached my ultimate goal?

_____

_____

_____

_____

_____

_____

_____

_____

LESSON ONE
EXERCISE 3

What do I value most? (If you enjoy writing and want to amplify this topic, you could add to it by saying how you exemplify your values daily.)

_____

_____

_____

_____

_____

LESSON ONE
EXERCISE 4

In reading Lesson One of the Book, what points did you pay particular attention to? Why?

Did any fears or joyful thoughts come up for you? What were they?

_____

_____

_____

_____

_____

By now, you have discovered that understanding *why you do something* can be as important as how you do it. When I know the motives behind my actions, it helps me to make the best plans possible to get what I want, to reach that dream. You may wish to skip right to the method of creating your specific plan of action beginning in Chapter 4.

However you wish to use this book is definitely your choice, and I hope that, at some point, you will give these exercises some of your attention.

Lesson Two

Bringing increased awareness to the Vision Mapping Strategies Process

Being yourself, in the jargon of today, might be called being *authentic* which simply means that the real you is showing up all the time. *Being yourself* means *living* your values, ethics, attitudes, and beliefs. When you live your daily life according to your own standards, you will be demonstrating who you are as a person, and that you can be trusted as being genuine. People will naturally want to be around you because they sense your confidence and self-assured manner. Basically, people want to feel loved… and they can experience that when you're authentic.

Here are some ways that I show up for others when I am authentic:

> - listening to what someone is saying and responding with honesty and compassion
> - appreciating the differences in others rather than judging
> - dealing with conflict calmly and intelligently
> - laughing a lot
> - being spontaneous and living in the present moment
> - having firm boundaries in place, saying "no" when it honors my integrity

Adults can tend to undervalue and not appreciate themselves. We all have significant attributes that can help others. So my theory is to recognize our own gifts and share them with others.

Julie's Story

Julie called me from the east coast. I didn't know her, but someone had referred her to me when I was living in Sedona. She wanted help with some major decisions. Her life had been revolving around caretaking too many people: her sister, her grown adult children, and even her supervisor at work.

She felt confused, alone, and frustrated – and knew that she was not living her life's calling. Counseling wasn't helping. She was ready to take the plunge into uncharted territory. By the time we finished our conversation, Julie had not made a commitment to come to Sedona to work with me, but she did email me several days later to say that even though she was very fearful of the outcome, she would spend time with me in Sedona.

Julie arrived, and we strolled the red dirt trails through an isolated Sedona canyon. After an hour of silence, she started crying. The red rocks were doing their magic, and Julie was letting go – of the confusion, heartache, and chaos that had settled in her heart for such a long time.

We completed Julie's visit with an extremely profound Vision Mapping process in which she laid out plans to become certified as a physical therapy assistant for physically handicapped children. Not only that, but she made a commitment to return to school and become a full-fledged physical therapist.

I haven't heard from Julie in a long time. I do know that when she left Sedona, she was radiant with joy and purpose, and ready to enroll in school to make her dream come true.

Knowledge is cumulative.

**One day, without expecting it, there is a realization that knowledge has provided the foundation for wisdom.
There is no doubt that our journey continually accumulates wise morsels that bring us a little closer to the true wisdom of ancient spirits, deepening our commitment to travel unknown depths in the quest for mysteries hidden in our souls.**

The stories and exercises in this Course are designed as tools for you to access a deeper level of your consciousness, to explore new possibilities and to discover how you can create your own perfect blueprint for the next steps of your journey in life.

**Vision + Passion + Focus + Action
= Abundance**

My secret for finding contentment in life is taking time to play. It has taken a long time to manifest a seamless life, as in: work is play, and play is work. My top activities are hanging out with my husband, adult sons, grandsons, and best friends. I love the beach, kayaking, photography, writing, traveling and African drumming. I'm also involved daily in work with developmentally disabled children and adults to support them in having the best quality of life possible.

Roadblocks

This next topic can be disguised in many ways. We may think that nothing can stop us from moving forward with our life plans. At least that's what I thought until I joined a *Tolerations* class with Thomas Leonard (who is widely considered to be the grandfather of professional coaching). In fact, what I learned about myself was so powerful that I completed this specific three month course on two separate occasions.

Simply said: there can often be obstacles that slow you down and prevent you from moving ahead at the speed of *you*. You may think that nothing hampers your journey to fulfillment, to your special goals… but think again. With some honest self-reflection you may discover some roadblocks in the way of your progress. Are you putting up with things in your life that are keeping you stuck? If so, what are they? What are all of your excuses for not manifesting your goal, your dream, your vision – not enough money, time, or energy?

Whoa! Turn the excuses around, and make a list of all the positive ways you can blast ahead. Listing them on paper will help you formulate a plan to eliminate them one by one so that there will not be *any more excuses* that keep you from reaching the success you envision. If you need help, reach out. You do not have to make this journey alone.

When I first worked on a Tolerations course with Thomas, I initially thought (very smugly, I might add) that nothing could slow me down. There was not one roadblock in my life. After sleeping soundly the night after our phone session, I woke up, grabbed pen and paper, and proceeded to fill out more than 27 things that I felt stood in the way of reaching my desired goals.

Obstacles that stood in my way included everything from a cluttered office to being too available for anyone who called and wanted help. One seemingly silly toleration that I had been putting up with for a long time was having paper clutter in front of my telephone. Every time the phone rang, I would look at the papers and sigh before I pushed them out of the way.

Sure, this was a pretty simple toleration and easy to eliminate, but the action of becoming aware and then doing something about it made a huge difference in my daily work. I wanted to ensure that I could find no excuses to keep me from reaching the goal I dreamed about, so I looked at all the snags in detail, and cleaned up the impediments one by one.

My Friend Anna

A much more challenging roadblock in my life involved a friend named Anna whom I had distanced myself from because she had become so demanding. Truth be told, she seemed to have developed increased emotional problems.

Anna began to call me at all hours of the day and early evening, expecting me to drop whatever I was doing and be present for her on the telephone. It took me awhile to realize that, in wanting to be supportive, I would stop what I was doing and listen to her litany of complaints.

Always being available to her wasn't helping either one of us, so I finally put some boundaries in place to eliminate the roadblock. The next time Anna called me, I told her I would be totally present and available to her — at a pre-scheduled time. She had several arguments about why this was not going to work for her. However, I was very clear that I would **only** be available at a time that we agreed upon, and if she called at other times I would remind her about our agreement and then end the conversation.

It took a few calls for her to realize that I was serious. Continuing to stand firm, by the fourth call we started having a meaningful hour long conversation weekly. Her call was expected, and I knew I could be totally present for her as I'd promised.

My point about the relationship with Anna is that some roadblocks can be transformed into workable solutions. Obstacles don't necessarily have to be eliminated. If the experience is very important to you, revamp it. In this case, I wanted to continue supporting Anna in ways that I could without being resentful, or getting frustrated or angry with her.

Now it's your turn to think about circumstances in your life and if any of them keep you going around in circles. This could involve people, places and/or things… anything that slows you down, gets in your way, or tries to derail you.

Remember that both roadblocks and tolerations are similar in that they prevent you from moving forward toward your goals. Reach deeply to think about things you are putting up with. When you start eliminating tolerations, you will begin to feel lighter.

It's time again to take what you've learned and work on some exercises. When you've completed those, continue to Lesson Three.

LESSON TWO
EXERCISE 1

Ways I show up for others are:

_____

_____

_____

LESSON TWO
EXERCISE 2

You've probably heard people talk about "being in the zone." To me, that phrase means that I'm in my own happy sphere, involved in doing something or being somewhere that I absolutely love. Time has no meaning. Pure joy engulfs me. My passion is unleashed. Well, ok, I don't mean to get carried away... but how many times in recent months (or years) have you felt wild abandonment? If my vision includes doing what I love to do – **and** I am in my passion every day – then I will be living my dream, my success.

Reconnect in your mind with those activities that take you to the **zone**. No one is going to see your writing but you, so don't hold back. Close your eyes if need be and call to mind the times in your life when you were living your bliss. Write whatever comes to you. Remembering and reconnecting the dots is very important as you begin to start forming your action plan.

LESSON TWO
EXERCISE 3

This is a playful exercise to create happiness awareness. **Carry a small notebook in your pocket** for at least two weeks. Every time you feel especially gratified, joyful, or just plain content, note the time and day, and write what you were actually engaged in and how it made you feel.

_____

_____

_____

_____

_____

The goal is to become more aware of how you are interacting with life and what creates excitement or serenity. There is no right or wrong in this exercise. Even if nothing makes you smile big, still it offers valuable information. After two weeks, take a good look at what you've jotted down and be observant of:

> - Patterns of behavior related to happiness
> - People who made you happy, and why
> - Situations which provided bliss (or simply feelings of fulfillment)
> - Days or times of the week that provided consistent joyful moments

TIPS:

Make a list of everything cheerful that you discovered through this exercise and keep it handy so that you can look at it every day. The idea is to continually reinforce your feelings of pleasure and well-being as you continue to complete your goal. It might be helpful to use the same *happiness* notebook to record any kind of obstacle you encounter, and later jot down if you notice any similarities among places, situations, or people.

LESSON TWO
EXERCISE 4

List any activity, person, or thing (no matter how minor) that might keep you stuck as you proceed toward your own goal. Keep in mind that some barriers might take weeks, months, or even years to clear. The immediate goal is to create awareness first, and then take action while on this journey. Be honest with yourself and explore possibilities.

After you complete your list, are you willing to make a mini-plan for eliminating each of them, one by one? Perhaps you can note the roadblock on the left side, and on the right side note two or three things that you could do to shift gears.

_____

_____

_____

_____

_____

LESSON TWO
EXERCISE 5

Now is a good time to review what you learned as you sharpened your self-perceptions. Here are some questions to ask yourself:

Were there any big surprises? If so, what were they?
Did you feel particularly motivated about any topic in particular? Explain.
Was there a significant shift in your thoughts about directions you are pursuing? If so, explain.

_____
_____
_____
_____
_____
_____

Review of Lesson Two

In Lesson Two you learned about:

- creating clarity
- showing up (how we show up for others)
- being aware of what makes you happy
- recognizing things that stand in your way (roadblocks)
- inspiration for you to take the next step
- making a mini-plan to eliminate each item in your life that keeps you stuck

When you finish reading about 'digging deeper into who you are' in Lesson Three, return to these questions and take time to write down your progressively deeper thoughts.

_____

_____

_____

_____

_____

_____

Lesson Three

Digging Deeper into Who You Are in Preparation for Your Action Plan

Questions can probe our thoughts in order to ponder our lives at a deeper level. Responses come from within, helping to guide us into the future. It would be easy for someone to just tell you what to do; however, you are the only one who truly knows what brings you happiness and feelings of completion and satisfaction. Sometimes, we even forget what happy or joyful feels like, and that's okay.

It's important to accept ourselves where we are in life, trusting that our growth is always perfectly timed. If you're not feeling quite confident enough about stepping out to make your dream come true, share it only with people who are supportive of you: friends, family, co-workers, and others who applaud who you are.

Recognizing Strengths

Sometimes we forget what we're really good at. We all admit that we are capable of many things, but we don't acknowledge them with celebration. Don't be shy. This is the time to think and act big. Playing small does not suit you on this journey. Do you have super strengths? For instance:

- being a very creative photographer who specializes in young children's photography
- having a natural talent for making people feel comfortable and at ease
- possessing organizational skills that are the envy and admiration of many people
- expressing compassion through volunteering for community activities

If you don't know what your unique gifts are, contact your friends and ask them what they think is special about you. Write everything down and bask in the light of their responses. Perhaps there is a personal trait that you have thought about but didn't consider as a possible topic to weave into your vision. **This is your time to think boldly and accept all those compliments and applause.**

Always remember to be kind to yourself. There are many people in the world who need to make you feel *less than* so they can feel *more than*. Remember to surround yourself with loving, supportive people.

Taking Care of Myself

If we're truly motivated to make our vision come true, we need to take care of ourselves on all levels. That means doing whatever you need to balance your life and create those relaxed times so that you can put intense energy into your strategies and your plan of action in order to reach that dream.

Excellent self-care could be anything from daily walks on the beach, to bubble baths and wine, to taking a weekend off and playing like you did when you were a kid. I have to admit that I need reminders to do this myself. It's easy to get in a rut and forget that we all need time off to rejuvenate – and I don't mean once a year. I'm talking weekly and even daily.

If we're committed to reaching the goal 100% of the time, the intense focus can lead to anxiety which is exactly what we **don't want.** Commitment to yourself and your vision takes many forms. Don't listen to anyone who says that you're being selfish because you are caring for yourself. You are the person who is going to make your dream come true.

Focus Fatigue

We all know how easy it is to get sidetracked while we're trying to stay focused on reaching our desired results. To eliminate **focus fatigue** or if you start to lose inspirational stamina, it will be helpful for you to assemble a few people who will champion your efforts.

When I began my coaching career, I thought this new journey would be a snap because I was always one of those natural cheerleaders who can sometimes drive a person crazy. However, I knew that on occasion my interest could wane even after a strong start, and the fabulous coaching program I had begun (CoachU) was going to consume much more time than I had originally envisioned.

Thomas Leonard recommended that I start my own advisory team, which I did. I called four friends: one in finance, a counselor, an entrepreneur, and a writer. Each of these people committed to talk with me once a week so that I could check in, be accountable to my process, and receive timely advice. I didn't call each of them every week, but I did call at least one of them every five to seven days. Having a supportive and loving team to count on helped me to keep my focus as I worked through the program, which took me about two years.

This is an excellent time for you to assemble your own advisory team as a squad of helpers on the journey towards your goal. If possible, include people with various expertise who are able to add specialized information if needed.

Surround yourself with positive people – those who truly wish for your success, and who will support you all the way to the finish line.

Life is too short to be slowed down by negativity.

It's always a good idea to thank people who help you along the way. Here are a few ways you could reciprocate:

- Swap/barter your expertise.
- Cook dinner for your team, or treat them to lunch.
- If a team member has small children, offer to babysit.
- Give them a gift certificate to their favorite store.
- Offer your expertise in a group telephone call.

Animal Crackers

Let me share a story about one of the most important telephone calls of my personal marketing education.

Many years ago my husband's and my fledgling record label (Nature Recordings/World Disc Music) had little marketing money, and I needed to be especially creative about ways to sell our CD products. Although we didn't realize it at the time, we were pioneering the concept of playing and selling music in the gift industry (i.e. Smithsonian Institute, Knott's Berry Farm, Monterey Bay Aquarium, Hallmark stores, Busch Gardens, nature store chains, health food stores etc.).

Attending and taking orders at wholesale trade shows was fun, and stressful. As we were getting ready to introduce our sixth CD (The Jungle) at a major gift show, I remembered **Animal Crackers** and thought how effective they could be for bringing buyer's attention to our product. I had already decided to dress up in safari clothes. And then came the idea to staple a tag around the string handle on the animal cracker box to let people know where they could locate our new product.

With pounding heart, I called Nabisco, the company which made them (coincidentally the company my dad worked for as a baker in Portland, Maine) and asked to speak with the marketing department. Someone came on the line and I asked how it would be possible to buy three cartons of animal crackers – wholesale.

There was silence on the other end of the phone. That person then turned me over to someone else, and then that person turned me over to yet another person. This went on for ten minutes. I'm sure that no one but retail dealers or sales people had ever contacted Nabisco for such a request, especially since I wouldn't be ordering again.

The last person who came on the line was a Senior Vice President of Nabisco. I didn't know whether to laugh or cry. So I decided to just tell him honestly why I had called. He chuckled a bit, but took me very seriously. One comment led to another and we talked (mostly him) for an hour. He was so pleased to know that someone wanted his advice.

This call proved to me that successful people want to help others be successful, too.
It never hurts to ask someone a question.
All they can do is say "No."
Nothing ventured – nothing gained!

Maybe you won't be able to reach senior staff but my point is this: reach out to others to help you get where you want to go. "No" is just a word, and we don't need to take it personally. When I've found the courage to ask, I've almost always received a "Yes"… and some of my best education.

By the way, Nabisco contributed the cookies (for free) and

our first trade show in San Francisco was a resounding success. Well, I did have to go into the showroom halls and walk up to people with the packages and say things like: "You look like a cookies and milk person. Please come visit us in the showroom." It's amazing what you can do when you're motivated enough.

As you are becoming more clear and focused about what is important to you, be consistent in reaching out to others with expertise. They may be people you've never talked to, and you may shudder with anxiety even thinking about doing this. Honestly, I've been there and I understand. But I also know that our multi-million dollar record label would not have been a great success if I had not pulled my courage together and just dialed the number to Nabisco

I'll meet you back here after you've worked through the reflection questions for Lesson Three. They will help you uncover much about yourself that you have forgotten or put aside under obligations, responsibilities, and fears. This is all important information toward creating your Vision Map.

LESSON THREE

LESSON THREE
EXERCISE 1

My super-strengths are:

_____

_____

_____

_____

_____

_____

LESSON THREE
EXERCISE 2

Ways that I can take excellent care of myself (be sure to include the things you do now to take good care of yourself) are:

_____

_____

_____

_____

_____

_____

_____

LESSON THREE
EXERCISE 3

These are people I can call to be supportive of my goals. (It might be helpful to note ways they can support you, and/or their special skills):

_____

_____

EXERCISE 4

When I am ready for expert advice, I will contact

_____

_____

_____

and ask him/her about _____

_____.

EXERCISE 5

How did you (or what will you do to) reward yourself for completing your fieldwork?

_____

_____

_____

_____

_____

_____

What "self-care" action(s) did you take?
Have you recognized a shift or a transitional/transformational experience since you began the Course? If so, what was it?

Who did you call to ask to be on your support team? What was their reaction to your request?

Preparation for Lesson Four

Now that you have forged a strong container to hold your evolving plan of action, this is the time to bring out that easel pad of paper and the markers.

I encourage you to have plenty of writing/drawing room with which to experiment. It's like, literally, working outside of the box, not having restrictions about ideas. It's a way to look at your vision in a non-linear fashion instead of lining up things neatly in rows.

There is no set way to design your mapping. Look at the examples in this Course if you need ideas. See how I've built my own plan of action, and use that as a model. However, whatever works for you is the *right* way.

When you commence with your vision, I want you to go to the edge of your comfort zone. Unconsciously (and consciously) you will **think BIG and write BIG**.
I guarantee that having lots of space to play with will lend itself to colossal ideas. I hope you're getting excited now, because the actual Vision Mapping plan begins with Lesson Four.

This is especially juicy. Now that you have a more solid idea of what you want, and why, your plan evolves into actions.

Lesson Four

Creating the Actual Vision Map – First Steps

Now you are ready to begin an actual Vision Map of your own. It will be exciting, introspective, informational…and just plain fun!

Clear vision + focus + plan of action = a dream come true

You may have noticed that in slightly varying ways, I continually accentuate the formula of "**clarity, focus, perseverance, consistency, action**." Some people believe that all you have to do is think your way to success. This may have some validity, but for me it's just part of the picture.

Positive thought and intention must be integrated with practicality and action for the best outcome possible.

Being clear about the end result, staying in a confident mindset and following your own plan of action to reach that goal will bring success. Any entrepreneur can tell you that you need creativity, a plan, and consistent action steps to gain incomparable outcomes. So I keep reminding you to stay focused.

There are no right or wrong ideas, only your ideas. You are beginning to translate your thoughts into a visual representation which will then lead you into a specific plan of action. I encourage you to tape these completed pages on a wall where you can look at them every day. After all, this is **your** blueprint.

As you glance at the papers throughout the days and weeks ahead, you may notice things you wish to change, things you want to tweak or delete, or have new inspirations to add. Most importantly, if you look at them every day, they will keep you on track and help to keep your motivation high.

Using brainstorming ideas and mapping, I am going to take you step by step through a few pages so that you can get ideas about creating your own blueprint. This is only one example. Your map will emerge regardless of the visual concept that you choose. You can do this alone, or you can ask someone to be the questioner. That person might see some gaps in your narrative, or use their intuition to ask some leading questions which will open up even more inquiry for you.

I've completed countless Vision Mapping sessions internationally and in the United States, and each one is unique. The examples shown here will give you an indication about how free-form this process is.

When I was establishing these methods, I remember how nervous I was the first few times I worked through the process. The bottom line is to do whatever is comfortable for you – but remember that edge you might be avoiding… and go beyond it.

A side note about my easel papers: When I do Vision Mapping illustrations, it is my intention to be bold, to go with the flow of spontaneous creativity – not to be neat – though of course I want to be able to read and understand my own notes when I'm ready to calendarize the actual schedule and to-do items.

Before you begin, remember to take 15 or 20 minutes in order to shift from the chatter in your head to being in the present moment, as you concentrate on the vision you hold dear.

Now it's time to put your easel pad (or other large paper) in front of you with your favorite colored markers, and begin your own Vision Mapping Strategies evolution. This is the beginning of your visual adventure.

The entire mapping development is designed to bring clarity and focus to actualization.

The purpose of Vision Mapping is to allow for spontaneous creativity and clarity regarding the what, who and why of your goal before the how to do it.

Please note that I am using actual easel-sized paper and markers to illustrate each step of this process…just the way I am encouraging you to do. It might look a little messy at times. I purposely chose not to make a perfect computer worksheet. Sometimes when we write plans and goals in a linear, line by line fashion, we miss the excitement of creating something BIG and WONDROUS --- full of passion, out-of-the-box ideas.

I've discovered that using easel paper, with plenty of room to spread out, somehow gives us permission to be more expansive in our minds. These first examples of worksheets are meant to give a feeling of freedom that you can do anything. You will have plenty of time to transfer your ideas into that nice neat step-by-step plan of action. Right now, have fun, be wild. Write down anything that comes to mind. You can filter all those ideas later.

For better visuals of the worksheets, please go to www.SharonHooper.com/worksheets as they might not display properly depending on the device you are using. If you are reading the printed version the online worksheets in full color will add new dimensions to your own ideas.

Sheet #1: Write down what you desire as an end result, your goal.

When I created this map, my vision was to have international retreats up and running by June 1, 2018.

I could have added that "filled" to me meant from ten to twenty participants. (It helps to be as specific as possible). Don't censor yourself with this process. The pages are for your eyes only (unless you choose to place them where others can view them - friends or co-workers who will not judge you or make negative comments).

One of my clients taped his five pages to a wall where a few select, supportive friends could see them. He invited them to add input anywhere on the worksheets, and some of those additions became part of his strategic plan. Others who witness your map can get excited about your plan and sometimes provide valuable input and ideas.

As you continue working on these sheets, tape them on a wall where you can look at them often. Add descriptions or words and phrases or cross out any items that are peripheral or don't serve your area of focus. Think of it as your own personal GPS or map – just like what you'd follow to navigate the best route to a location you were seeking.

On the second sheet I added a few topics about the details of my goal. You will notice that I added Values at the bottom of the page. It is essential to continually remind yourself that however you manifest your goal, you must always keep in mind your values and priorities and the things that bring joy, honor and integrity into your life.

Becoming more specific about my vision

On the third sheet that follows, I added many more details: the topic of retreats, a rough concept of my marketing opportunities, locations for retreats, and my audience.

Sheet #2: Getting more detailed and focused

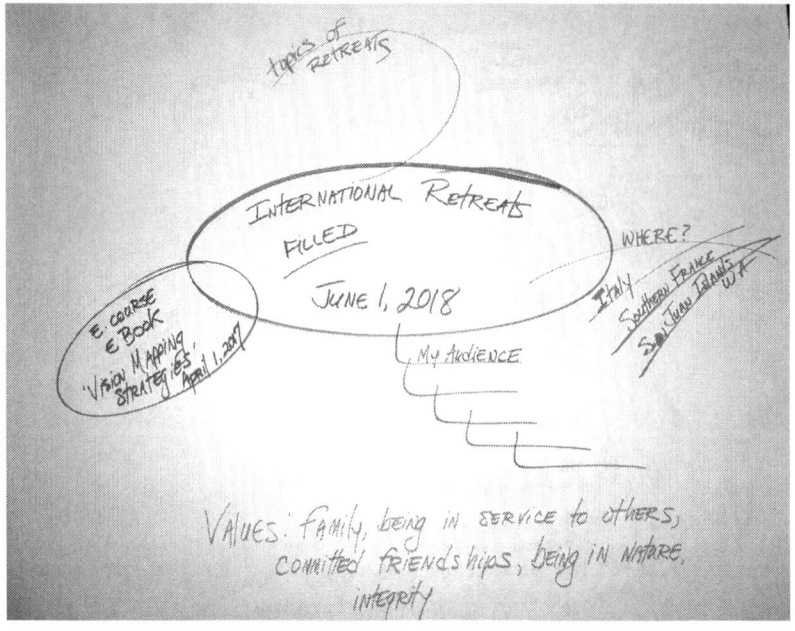

Recapping what I have written above on the map (clockwise from the top):

The **topics of retreats** are: personal development; creating clarity with ideas and goals; making plans of action; and, inspiring entrepreneurial businesses with ideas.

The **marketing plan**, or **how will I reach my audience**, consists of social media; blogging; swapping links; co-producing with someone.

Sheet #3:

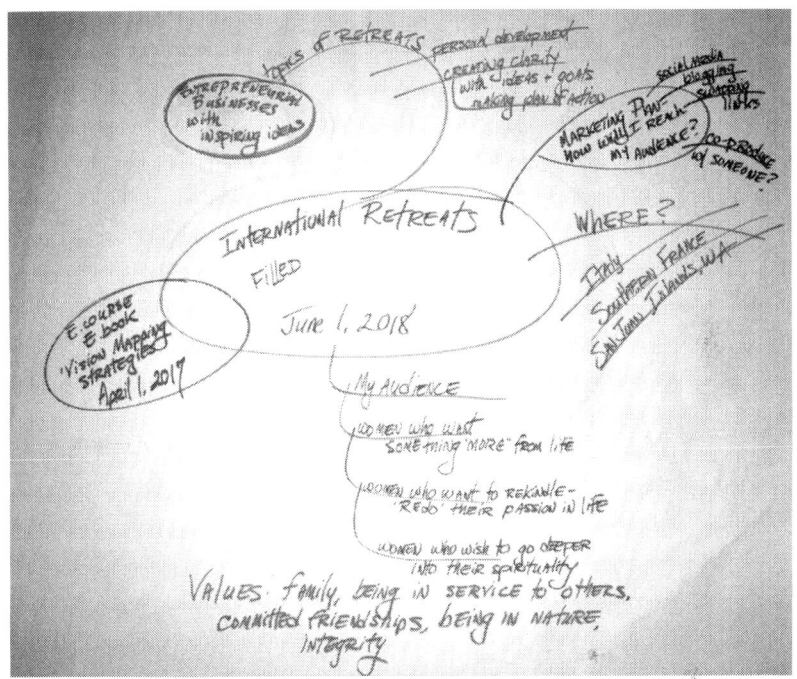

Where: Italy; Southern France; Sedona, Arizona; San Juan Islands, Washington.

Who do I want my retreats to reach?: Women who want something more from life; women who want to rekindle their passion in life; women who wish to go deeper into their spirituality.

Another goal that I'm working on simultaneously is: an eCourse/Book for *Vision Mapping Strategies*.

Added at the bottom are my values: family, being in service to others, committed friendships, being in nature and integrity. I didn't put this on the map, but I would like to add being part of something bigger than myself.

Remember that this is *your* process. Your map, or blueprint, will look totally different. My goal as a facilitator is to help you connect your heart and head with your visions or goals. Now is the time for you to step up to the next level – whatever that means to you.

If your creative juices haven't kicked in and you'd like some one-on-one coaching with your process, **get in touch with me** about a phone or Skype session. We can work together to coax a dream from the depths of your heart into a laser focus that can make your mapping and strategies more effective.

Bottom line: ***don't stay stuck.*** **If you're challenged by ideas, just keep filling up pages with whatever comes to mind. The perfect result will emerge, regardless of what your map looks like. Continue to move forward – not backwards or standing still. Have faith, trust, and courage in your own process. You already have everything you need to succeed in life and business.**

The following example is the first page by Maria, who is thinking about moving from Sydney, Australia, possibly to the Northwest. She did a Vision Mapping process with me from Australia via Skype.

Sheet #4: First page of Maria's Vision Mapping

Maria's first sheet showed the center as you see it here. Her goal was "Joy and passion for the day ahead and life ahead." She didn't have a particular end-date in mind. This process was simply part of her journey.

When we created her second sheet, we added all the other topics you see here: her skills, roadblocks she had identified, and an outline of her next steps. Together we eventually created a specific plan of action for her to pursue over the next two years.

Sheet #4:

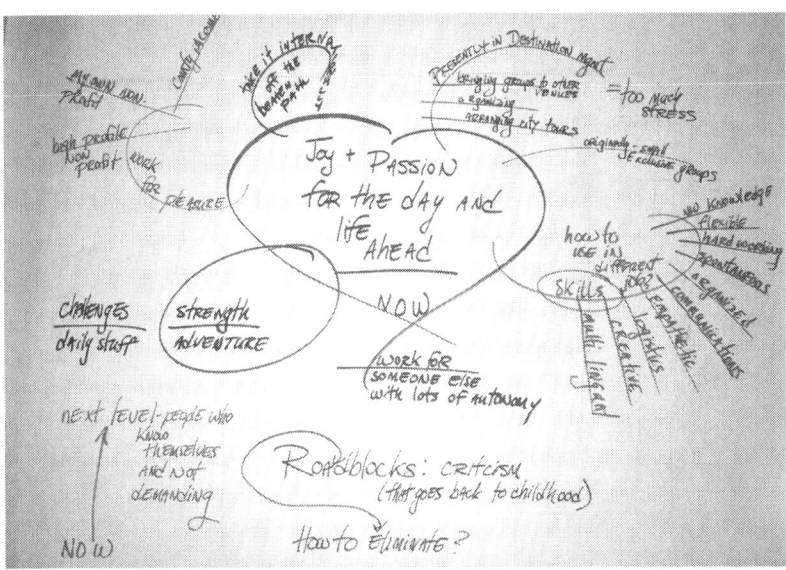

When we move on to Lesson Five, you'll see how your first maps can transition into explicit plans of action. But before we move on to explain how you can create a timeline which will lead you week by week to the results you desire, I have more reflection questions for you. After their completion, come back to the Book for Lesson Five.

LESSON FOUR
EXERCISE I

What was your biggest surprise in starting this Vision Map? Did your vision change from your original idea? If so, what changed?

Was there a stumbling block, a challenging thought perhaps, as you continued the mapping? What was it?

What, if any, excitement or mastery did you feel as you were working on this section of your Vision Map?

Did any doubts arise about your confidence while you were working on this portion of your map? Did you stop and wonder how you were going to combine your mapping ideas with your initial goal toward successful completion?

_____

_____

_____

_____

_____

_____

_____

_____

_____

Lesson Five

Action is the Key to Success

The fifth Lesson of our Course is where people can sometimes get stuck and might argue with themselves by thinking, "Well, I haven't been able to get this to work before, so why should I keep trying?" Figuring out the *how* to do things is almost always the most challenging aspect of goal planning.

_____

_____

_____

_____

_____

_____

_____

_____

_____

_____

_____

_____

_____

_____

Perhaps you have heard before that what you think about the most — what you pay attention to — often determines what actions you take.

I frequently remind myself to give consideration to my thoughts, lest they unexpectedly tempt me to wander onto a completely different path, one that is not focused on manifesting a specific vision.

What are you thinking right now? What kind of books or magazines do you read that inspire your path moving forward? Who are your friends that surround your life? Do all of them support your best efforts?

Maybe this is a perfect moment to take a quick inventory in your mind related to the above reflections. I'm not proposing that you have to be in perfect action all the time, nor change relationships with friends, family or co-workers.

Just take stock of what's up for you right now. And then make a determination about what, who, or where will best serve your passionate devotion to reach the dream or the goals you most desire.

_____

_____

_____

_____

_____

In fact, in the back of my head I can hear my own past agonies of, "Yeah, this is a great idea, but I don't know *how* to make it happen." I'm actually grinning and thinking about all the groanings I've heard from clients during my coaching and consulting career. I have to admit that when I created the process of Vision Mapping Strategies in the late 1990's, my own strategies changed continually until I felt that the concept was mastered.

So let's plot the steps to make it happen. To begin fabricating your own annual calendar, month by month, week by week, start with the following illustration. (You'll note that I'm still using my own International Retreats Goal calendar as our example).

First, **let's review the third map again**. (on page 49) Note the *who, what, where* questions I answered, and the inclusion of my values as a reminder.

In the next worksheet, I'm transitioning from the free-form vision of my map to a definitive calendar.

Again, use a large sheet of paper which will give you lots of playing room. When the action plan is complete, you can create the linear outline if you wish.

_____

_____

_____

_____

_____

Sheet #5: Narrowing the times that I can utilize to work on my plan

As you can see, I've roughly laid out a calendar for one year. I started backwards from the date of completion I had in mind. The numbers 1 – 4 beneath each month represent one week each.

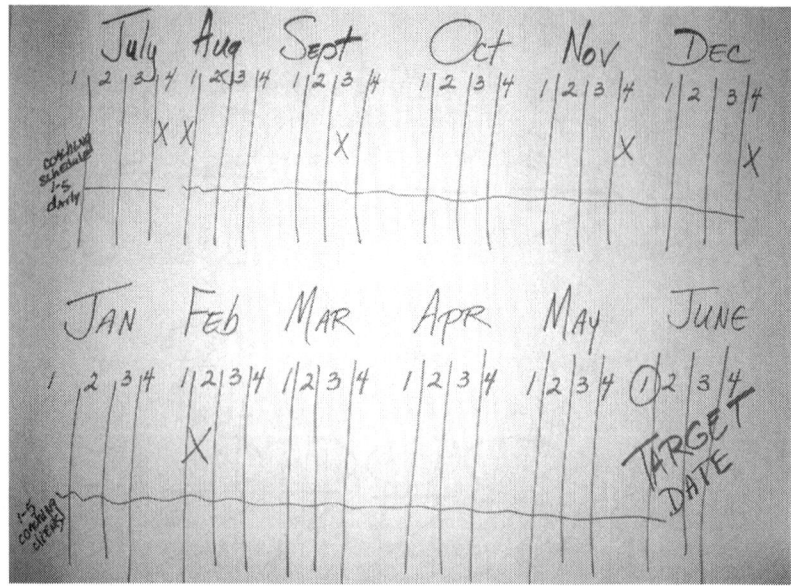

In order to plan a specific framework of time for this work in progress, I need to cross out dates that I consider to be non-negotiable. There are activities that will make me unavailable to work on my master action plan. For instance, the 4th week of July and the 1st week of August I will be out of town. The 3rd week of September and the 4th week of November are also fully booked.

You can see that I've added coaching clients to my afternoon commitments.

I can now plan available slots of time to consistently work toward the accomplishment of my goal. I've discovered that most people (including myself) have great intentions to complete plans – but life often gets in the way. By constructing a calendar for myself I'll ensure that I'm on target to reach my desired result, in the time frame I've projected.

Sheet #6: Building your calendar in order to reach your goal's target date

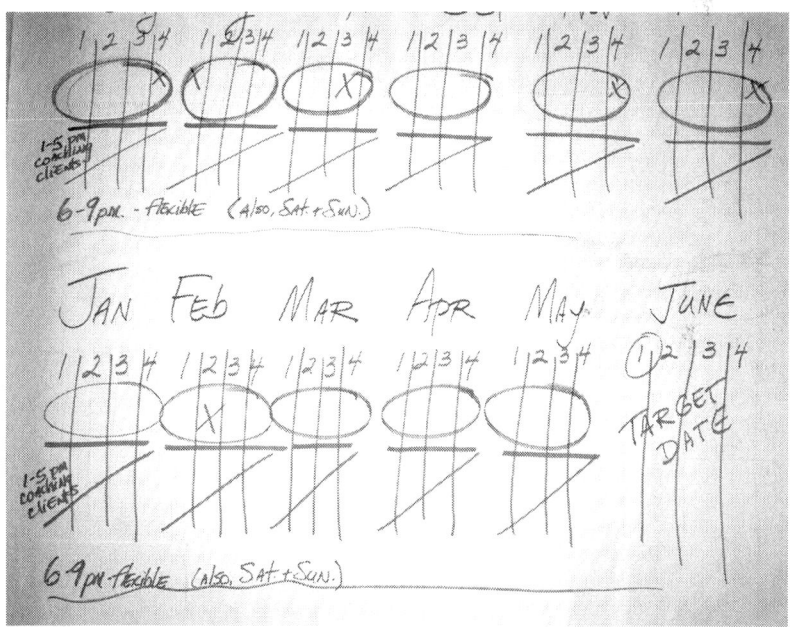

On this sheet I've crossed through the times that I'm not available (in the afternoons) to work on my targeted action plan – blocks of time for other paid work, travel dates, or anything that has been scheduled in advance that generally cannot be altered.

You can see that every afternoon from 1 – 5 is set aside for coaching calls. The "Xs" are weeks that I will not be working. Theoretically, the times I have available to concentrate on my plan of action are mornings from 8 a.m. to noon (five days a week), all day Saturday and Sunday and every evening between 6 and 9 p.m.

For simplicity, I haven't blocked out a few various appointments or my daily walking times. I now have ample time to assign myself tasks as I move forward to fill my international retreats by June 1, 2018.

Sheet #7:

The details start filling in.
This map looks rather busy. If you continue reading below, I have explained each month (neatly) according to what I have written on this map.

So far, you have:

* created clarity on your vision, goal, or desired result
* reached deeper into your mind and heart to focus on your passions and strengths
* added interests/skills/ideas to your map
* drawn a general calendar for one year and filled in "must do's"

Take a few minutes to review your compelling goal. Now we start digging down into the guts of how you will make things happen.

I've added monthly steps, and started backwards from my completion date. For instance, June 2018 is the target month for retreat in Italy, so looking at what needs to be accomplished each month prior in order to make that happen, I added the following. (Yes, it *is* getting busy… and that will change soon).

_____

_____

_____

_____

_____

_____

_____

1. End July 2017 - Complete research for lodging, all costs, and rough itinerary; Start blogging about Italy.

2. End August 2017 - Itinerary/flyer out to my mailing lists, on Facebook, Twitter, LinkedIn; Feature discounted price that expires in February.

3. September 2017 - Blog about Italy (including pictures); Continue with Facebook and Twitter blurbs, but don't overdo it.

4. October 2017 - Continue with marketing efforts.

5. Mid-November 2017 - Send flyer/itinerary to mailing lists again; Continue with marketing.

6. Mid-December 2017 - Blog about winter holidays in Italy; Continue with marketing.

7. January 2018 - Continue blogging about Italy; Include ways that my retreat's topic of Vision Mapping Strategies is beneficial.

8. **February 2018** - Send flyer again (last chance for discount).

9. **March 2018** - continue to market/blog.

10. **April 2018** - Conference call with attendees; Continue to market through social media.

11. **May 2018** - 2nd conference call with attendees; Send specific and updated schedule.

12. **June 2018** - Off we go!

Clients usually tell me they don't have time to do everything.

EXACTLY!

This is why you have to decide who and what is most important in your life and make decisions which will bring you ecstatic results.

And yes, you may have to sacrifice some activities in order to make your dream happen.

Lesson Five may have taken you several hours, or perhaps only 45 minutes. For me, this is always the most challenging piece because I'm interested in so many things – but I knew that I had to get totally clear and committed if I wanted my retreats to happen. However, I also knew that whenever I am 100% involved in manifesting a vision, I am always successful.

It took me about three hours to carefully plot a one year course of action. It wasn't just filling in blanks. I had to get in touch with both my mind and my heart about what I wanted to accomplish, and realistically outline exactly *how* I was going to carve out the time to meet my desired goal. My still-rough plan dictated that I would have to forfeit some activities for the next year. I knew for sure that if I was committed to a goal, I would have to rethink the immediate future because there wasn't enough time in the day to accomplish everything.

**Keep up your energy, creativity,
and game plan as you move along.**

**If you need support or feel as if you're
lagging, bring your advisory team together.**

or email me at Sharon@VisionJourneys.com

**Reward yourself for the astounding
blueprint that you are directing.**

**Persistence + action + stamina
= DREAM COME TRUE**

**And at all times practice being
in the present moment.**

The next part of the Course is going to transform your free-form design into a more linear outline of your *to-do* list. Continue to use easel paper as you build your list until (and if) you're ready to transfer your agenda to a smaller, manageable size of paper.

LESSON FIVE
EXERCISE

While making a calendar of the time you will devote toward reaching your goal, what did you discover about your personal work habits and/or life schedule? Were you excited about making a specific plan to manifest your vision or goal? Did you throw up your hands in dismay because you try to fit in too many activities each week?

What kinds of **sacrifice** or **change** of plans did you make? How has your goal or dream changed since you began the first Lesson? Was calendarizing your vision easy for you, or challenging? Why?

_____

_____

_____

_____

_____

Congratulations on sticking with the Course and working through these exercises! You have uncovered and discovered so much toward the creation of *your* Vision Map – the blueprint that can truly help you make your dreams and goals a reality.

You can always revisit the exercises at a future date to see how much you've grown and changed – or to help you map another inspired vision. **Now**, *let's move on to Lesson Six.*

Lesson Six
Carrying Out Your Action Plan

With Lesson Six we start getting down to the foundation of making this dream happen. This is when you get to plan the time each day that you will devote to your commitment.

This is the same worksheet as in lesson five, sheet #7. I am including it here again for illustrative purposes.

On the next sheet I've transferred my July through September to-do list from this larger schedule above. I've decided to devote two hours every day (first thing in the morning, while my energy is high) to working methodically on the plan to accomplish my end goal in June 2018.

By the end of July I'll have a rough draft of the retreat flyer. By the end of August, the flyer will be disseminated via social media, friends, and other sources. In September, I will continue marketing the retreats through various means and will hold a conference call for anyone who would like to talk about Italy in general and/or share their Italy travel experiences.

You can also break the months into weekly plans. For instance, the first two weeks in July I plan to concentrate on locating the specific venue to hold the retreats. The third week's target is to tabulate all the costs in order to prepare the flyer's rough draft, which I will complete during the last week of July.

During the following months I will concentrate on marketing the retreats. Discounts will be offered until the end of February 2014. In April and May, I will hold teleconferences for the attendees to help us all prepare for the retreat in June.

Sheet #8:

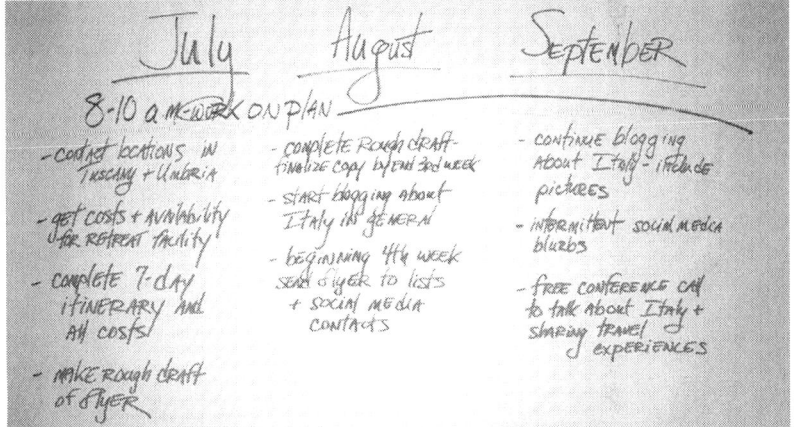

Review of Lesson Six

You laid out the timeline of your commitment to complete each piece of your action plan. You're now dedicating your valuable time and energy to reach a specific goal.

When your vision was a thought or idea in your mind, there was no real commitment to make it happen. Many times people procrastinate for months or years – even sometimes decades – because they fear that if they actually take steps to make their dream happen, it might fail.

However, as someone who invested in this Course, you have made a commitment to yourself to make your vision materialize. Time is precious, and you deserve to be living your dream.

When each facet of your plan is completed, in a relatively brief period of time you will have reached the goal or vision that you've been dreaming about.

With the tools you now have, you are able to define each task clearly so that you won't have to waste time rethinking each process every day. Before you know it, you will be months into your timeline – and that much closer to your goal.

Personally, I've found that making a list at the end of each week helps me accomplish a lot more. When Monday rolls around, I know exactly what I need to do. Looking back over the history of my work in many arenas, I can envision what it looked like "with lists" and "without lists."

I know for a fact that when I made lists and followed them, I accomplished at least 25% or more during that week. Of course that gave me more time to play, which was – and is – very important to me. Maybe it is for you, too. Balance is always a good thing.

Afterword

Review and Coordination of Vision/Goal Implementation

Some of these Lessons might have seemed particularly challenging to you. Others may have been a snap. For me, the most difficult part of the journey is always gaining clarity about what I want to accomplish.

Sometimes the newness of an idea inspired me to get halfway through my own process of defining and making action plans, and then I lost interest and went on to something else. I had to be truly committed to the essence of a project to carry it through to completion.

When I worked for DOD (Department of Defense) there were expectations and goals already in place. However, within those parameters there was always something new that I could implement, and many times a better way to manifest the desired end result.

Knowing what inspires and motivates you, and what you are passionate about, is crucial to the success of your goal. During those years before the music business, I had no idea that I was an **entrepreneur** until my work birthed a record label. When my husband Richard started nagging me about selling his pure nature sounds, my first question was, "Why would anyone buy those?"

Yet millions of dollars later, we had discovered that museums, entertainment parks, and gift stores in general were interested in them. Just about every age group, both male and female, wanted to buy the CDs. Bored with too many confines, I was finally ready to spread my wings and take some calculated risks. And those risks paid off.

Incorporating your values into daily work will create the impetus to make your vision or goal come true.

Forcing yourself to do something you have little interest in, stifles *the true you* who wants to live your dream.

I've presented you with a lot of information. Working through it should help you gain clarity and focus. The creation of your month by month calendar can assist you in making your goal a reality. I hope that you have a better understanding of how fear can hold you back by throwing continual roadblocks on your path.

Courage + persistence + commitment + consistency + patience with self + action = abundance and success

Even if you haven't begun your actual plan yet, you have gained momentum and re-aligned your passion with the motivation to implement what it takes to make that dream happen. Though we all move forward at our own pace while honoring our process, it's also crucial to continue taking one step after another to reach the results we desire.

And, as we know, life is subject to change – sometimes often. So remember: on your road to the life of your dreams, allow yourself flexibility, compassion, patience, courage, and a strong dose of intuition.

And if you're ever in need of some encouragement or help in clarifying your vision or goal, email me at Sharon@VisionJourneys.com and we'll work together to get you on track.

May you be blessed with joyful abundance, and may you experience the enlivening of your dreams and the successful achievement of your goals!

Sharon

Courage + persistence + commitment + consistency + patience with self + action = Unconditional and absolute SUCCESS!

Books and Resources to Support Your Journey

Now that you have completed the Course and know how to create your own *Vision Mapping Strategies*, I'd like to share some books and magazines that helped me to be successful in many endeavors and situations in life. Perhaps they will become some of your own new favorites.

But before listing titles of books and other resources that I found to be invaluable support on my journey, let me tell you a bit about how I came to adopt *"You do what you need to do until you don't need to do it anymore"* as my basic philosophy in life. Maybe doing so will spare you some of the snags and delays I encountered, and put you on a fast track in reaching the goal(s) for which you utilize *Vision Mapping Strategies.*

I found this adage simultaneously easy to grasp, yet challenging to understand – I didn't even get it until around my late 40's. For instance, saying to myself that I was going to lose thirty pounds sounded easy, but consciously accomplishing that (or any) goal could have meant a year or more of false starts, wasted energy, re-do's, discouragement, and frustration with myself over a lack of focus, concentration, and/or discipline.

However, when I created *Vision Mapping Strategies* in 1999 (using myself as a guinea pig) the goals became easier to reach as I discovered and strategized steps leading to the completion and successful conclusion of whatever my desired accomplishment happened to be.

One day when I was traveling to a gift trade show in Atlanta, I was browsing the airport book store and the first issue of **Fast Company** magazine caught my eye. After I bought it and read through every page, that periodical became my most important idea generator. I was enthralled with all the progressive ideas and energy that came pouring out of the articles. If you try out a few issues you may become hooked in the exciting and trendy monthly articles.

Inc. Magazine was also an ideal periodical to discover what was happening in the business world. In fact, our record label, World Disc Recordings, was a finalist two years running during their annual awards for the best and most innovative companies in the United States.

These two magazines especially sparked new visions in my head, and I used my Yankee ingenuity to transform their ideas into what might work for our burgeoning international record label. Our staff grew from two to thirty-two people and ten international recording artists who were signed to our label. The record label provided my own playground to experiment with new ideas – especially in the marketing arena.

Two of the most motivational books that entered my life were *Susan Jeffers' Feel the Fear and Do It Anyway* and *Dr. Robert Schuller's The Peak to Peek Principle: How Possibility Thinkers Succeed*. Jeffers' words guided me through several scary situations, and I have used these phrases with many friends and clients. In my own words, it's simply this:

Fearful thoughts and emotions can surface weekly, more or less.

Acknowledging the fear is important. However, we don't need to let fear slow us down. We can feel that fear and still go on with life.

Simply take the fear, stick it inside your invisible pocket, thank it for teaching you… and **act anyway**, knowing that fear is present to teach you about your own life and how to stand strong and courageously as you walk forward on your path. That said, I don't expect any of us to take unwarranted risks that can damage our bodies or our minds.

It's important to know the difference between fears *keeping you stuck* versus *fears warning you* about something dangerous or too risky. If you're in doubt, reach out to someone and talk about your own specific situation to ensure that you make the very best decision – for YOU.

I discovered Dr. Robert Schuller's book by accident. (Well, actually, I don't believe in accidents.) When I was making one of those life-changing transitions and didn't know where to turn or the best steps to follow, this book somehow came into my line of sight.

The messages he delivered gave me the courage to go on, creating small goals every month. The small goals eventually turned into reaching the outcome I was facing: a path that was extremely fearful to me, and yet one that I knew had to be walked if I was ever going to possess the strength I admired in other women. Dr. Schuller's ideas supported me in making necessary (and huge) transitions.

The other books that I include here have been truly instrumental along my path. Some of them may not seem like your ordinary business books, for I discovered that inspirational reading helped me to unlock my creative superpowers – whether for entrepreneurial ventures, or taking that next quantum leap into the fray of what we call an "educated emotional risk." This list does not contain all the books which have inspired or encouraged me, but I think a good sampling. These are listed in alphabetical order by the author's last name.

Zen and the Art of Making a Living: A Practical Guide to Creative Career Design by Laurence G. Boldt

> "Over a number of years, I worked to develop such a program. Its purpose is to enhance human creativity in work, and in so doing, to assist people to experience the full joy of living. It has three ingredients: a spiritual or mythic approach to life in general and work in particular, an emphasis on service, and freedom of choice."

This introduction of his book spoke strongly to me. I carried the 600-page book everywhere and read a few pages at every spare moment. Here it was: exactly how I wanted to build a career, and business – practically, creatively and spiritually. Someone had written on the back cover, "Everyone is the artist of his or her own life." And so I began to create my own new and revised canvas. The year was 1991, and I gave myself permission to intuitively follow each new step as it arose in my mind. I rediscovered exactly what "following my own path" meant… so I did exactly that, and was guided to create that multi-million dollar record label.

Everyday Sacred: A Woman's Journey Home by Sue Bender

> "… Like the monk going out with his empty bowl, I set out to see what each offered. I began noticing, the way an observer might, what I was doing – all my thoughts, feelings, and experiences that might be connected to everyday sacred. Somehow, in some way not yet shown to me, I felt there was a connection between EVERYDAY SACRED and the BEGGING BOWL."

Karen Ely, Founder of The Sedona Women's Institute, gave me a scholarship to attend a weekend retreat given by Ms. Bender in Sedona, Arizona. Attending this gathering provided a huge transformational shift in my life: what or who did I want to **consciously attract every day?**

A week after the retreat, I found a special small bowl and kept it on my kitchen counter. Every morning this container reminded me to ask myself, "What am I going to put in my bowl today?" The bowls I used have changed through the years; presently the eight-inch round container with a lovely lid respectfully infers that I may be a little rounder at this stage of my life. Yet it too still begs the question, "With what will I fill my bowl today?"

It prompts me to do a short meditation with my hands wrapped around that symbolic bowl. Those three to five minutes in the morning help center me for the day ahead.

A Retreat of My Own by Karen Ely

> "It's time to pause. It's time to step back. It's time to put away your long to-do list, find a quiet pace, put on some gentle music… pull out your journal and

take the first step back to yourself. For it is only in the quiet that we hear the stirring of our own hearts."

I love giving and attending women's retreats. I've participated in many, from the wilds of Montana canyons to the warmth of summer beaches in Maine to Sedona's majestic red-rock canyons. After reading this gem, I realized that it's very rewarding to physically journey to retreats. And in between those times, Ely's heartfelt description of her life's path, along with the tips and exercises she provides, re-inspired me to take time for myself and reflect on how I am living my life. If you are longing for a space just to be *you*, regardless of where you are, this guide will help you uncover the mysteries of your deepest self – whether you are sitting under a tree in the park or curled up in your favorite nook at home. Perhaps Ely's dedication to the book says it all: "Dedicated to women who dare to dream…"

Enduring Lives: Portraits of Women and Faith in Action by Carol Lee Flinders

> "All the women in this book have had to contend with firestorms of absolutely legitimate anger, and every one of them has made an angel of her anger: not a saccharine little feather-winged wisp of a thing but a fierce seraphim with a sword. An angel nonetheless, tender and unyielding at once, and magnificently effective."

Ms. Flinders' portraits of Sister Helen Prejean, Jane Goodall, Etty Hillesum and Tenzin Palmo inundated me with feelings that I didn't even know existed. I held my breath as I read their stories and cried with joy when outcomes were revealed. For female spiritual seekers, the stories of these contemporary women will inspire you to reach even deeper into your own well of strength as you walk your transformational path.

The E-Myth Revisited: Why Most Small Businesses Don't Work and What to Do About It by Michael E. Gerber

> "The dream of American Small Business… A world of our own… It's a yearning for structure, for form, for control. Something less distinct, yet much more intimately connected with who we are as human begins. It's a yearning for relationship with ourselves and the world in a way impossible to experience in a job."

Mr. Gerber supplied the concept that in any job I held, whether working for the government or being president of my own company, I had to fill that integral personal yearning for meaning. My goals have never been to make lots of money, but to help improve the lives of others through whatever means were available to me. And somewhere along the way, I had faith that I would be taken care of. Even in my darkest moments I was always given the support and courage to come through a tunnel into the light.

Take Off Your Pants! Outline Your Books for Faster, Better Writing by Libbie Hawker

I'm a writer. It could be about business, spirituality or my grandchildren. For two years I wrote a regular column for United Press International's online spirituality and religion site. A few years ago I published a book called "**Avalon Rose, First Blush.**" It got outstanding reviews, and then I didn't do anything about marketing it; and and the book languished in storage room boxes. ("**Avalon**" will become an ebook soon.)

In late 2016, Libbie (an extremely successful ebook writer) came into my life and encouraged me to upload Avalon to Kindle and also introduced me to her book about outlining. If you have a fiction novel rolling around in your head, *you must order this book!*

"Libbie's no-nonsense advice and specific how to write your outline will make your writing life so much easier. *Take Off Your Pants!* is a guide to help you increase your speed and efficiency as an author. It will provide you with a method for planning out a book's particulars before you begin to write - and a method for ensuring that your book will be cohesive, compelling, and satisfying." (www.LibbieHawker.com)

The voice of **Thich Nhat Hanh** is one I treasure. A Zen Master, global spiritual leader, poet and peace activist, he is revered around the world for his powerful teachings and bestselling writings on mindfulness and peace. He teaches that, through mindfulness, we can learn to live happily in the present moment - the only way to truly develop peace, both in oneself and in the world. With over 100 titles to choose from, his words can be at your desk and bedside offering gentle wisdom and encouragement to begin, punctuate, and end your day.

The Direct Path: Creating a Personal Journey to the Divine Using the World's Spiritual Traditions by Andrew Harvey

> "...The best way...around your evolving divine self is by devoting yourself, as quickly and consistently as possible, to prayer, meditation, the study of spiritual

and mystical texts and systems, and the cultivation of compassion, patience, humility, and generosity in all your practical choices in life and all your dealings with others."

I found that following Mr. Harvey's directions called for great discipline and cultivation, which I have to admit have often been very challenging for me. As it did for Mr. Harvey, whispering the prayer of St. Francis seems to ground me when I am being pulled away from my inner compass by the challenges of everyday life.

> Lord, make me an instrument of thy peace.
> Where there is hatred, let me sow love.
> Where there is injury, pardon.
> Where there is doubt, faith.
> Where there is despair, hope.
> Where there is darkness, light.
> Where there is sadness, joy.
>
> O Divine Master, grant that I may not so much seek
> to be consoled as to console,
> to be understood as to understand,
> to be loved as to love.
> For it is in giving that we receive.
> It is in pardoning that we are pardoned.
> It is in the dying to self that we are born to eternal life.

Jesus, Buddha, Krishna, & Lao Tzu – The Parallel Sayings **by Richard Hooper**

"The goal of all mystical paths is to recognize oneness with God, or whatever one chooses to call Ultimate Reality. We are told by spiritual teachers that we already are One, we just don't realize it.

In reality, there is nothing to achieve, nothing to become, nothing to do… but wake up! And to wake up, all we have to do is clean our doors of perception, which will easily and automatically allow us to become aware of our essential unity with All-That-Is."

The way in which these teachings are presented answered many questions for me. The columns of parallel meanings guided my understanding of how the great mystics of all traditions conveyed a commonality of spiritual truths.

I love the intuitive insight and wisdom of **Caroline Myss,** and find anything she produces to be of real value. She has a wide selection of books, audios, and videos (http://www.myss.com/product-category/offsite-products/) on a variety of subjects: soul contracts, archetypes, personal and energetic healing, and self-esteem, to name a few – all well worth your time.

I hope the voices of these authors (as well as those of your own favorites) inform and support your inner voice in mapping your visions to bring your dreams to life.

Elinor Stutz

Elinor and I have been each other's gurus for several years. We are able to speak our pure truth with each other, share wacky ideas, and we totally concur about integrity with sales and marketing. She has written several books, and I especially love her latest, *The Wish – A 360 Degree Business Development Process That Fuels Sales.*

The Wish is essential for entrepreneurs and business owners of all sized companies. Everything Elinor learned from her professional sales career as a top producer to becoming a top 1% influencer, according to Kred, is shared in this new book. Personal stories, including tough lessons, are included to use as examples and for entertainment also, like: putting sales on a higher plane, social media strategies and converting effort directly to sales. Recently, she was listed as one of the "Top 65 Business Women". You can find out more about Elinor at www.smoothsale.net

-If you have a special recommendation, please feel free to share it with me.

Sharon

Inspirations and Considerations

Please continue reading the following questions and responses on topics I frequently receive from people about new business challenges, getting stuck in life, and how to stay motivated.

Perhaps you have a similar circumstance and the inquiries will provide ideas for your next steps forward. If you have a question, please email me.

Dear Coach Sharon,

> There are so many things I want to do. I'm already too busy for my own good, but I don't seem to be accomplishing what really matters to me. I want to do something new, a dream I've had for ten years, and I just can't seem to get started. I know that I often keep going in circles. My Buddhist friends tell me that I haven't "awakened" yet. What the heck does that mean, and how do I get started? Challenged in Oregon

Dear Challenged,

My philosophy has been simple for years - **We do what we need to until we don't need to do it any more**. Sounds easy, right? The challenge is in knowing how to make the changes when we realize that we're ready to shift. Of course, becoming awake is not effortless either.

I am not an expert on spiritual or religious traditions. However, there is an overriding concept called "mindfulness," (frequently associated with Buddhism) which I began practicing twenty years ago. Mindfulness has helped me gain an inner calm and knowing. I certainly cannot claim to have awakened, but somewhere along the way, confused thoughts have become more clear and created a course of deeper understanding through my practice of being mindful.

This is a path for anyone, an approach that may help you to define what is most important in your life and consequently lead you to manifesting your dream. **Mindfulness** practice and training has become quite popular over the last few years. You will be able to find multitudes of information about this on the internet.

From a coaching perspective, let's discuss how you might become more attentive and aware of what is happening around you. When you make a commitment to be watchful of your thoughts and actions, I believe that unnecessary pursuits and strivings will drop by the wayside. Simultaneously, you will naturally begin adopting new practices in your life that will result in some surprising directions.

This is just one way to begin your exercise in being more aware of what is happening in your life. For three or four weeks (or longer if you wish):

1. Carry a small pad of paper around with you - everywhere.

2. Jot down a phrase or even a full page of writing whenever you feel excited and happy by something. What is it that suddenly impressed you?

3. Use just one word…or quickly describe the circumstances of the episode. Your ultimate task in this activity is to be particularly observant of your thoughts.

4. Write any spontaneous ideas that surface before you close and put away this pad…for the time being.

Now, take another fresh notebook and carry it with you for a few weeks.

1. Write down words or thoughts about things, circumstances or people that you feel drained by. Perhaps something saddens you. Make a note of this also.

2. If you wish, use this same pad to be aware of when you are doing **busy work**. This may be too much for you to do at one time, so just be aware of what feels most comfortable to you while you are exploring. (However, you know that I love stretching until we move out of our comfort zone.)

3. Practice being alert throughout this assignment. The object is to capture specific types of feelings.

After you have completed this series of being watchful, take out the first memorandums and highlight the most important words or phrases. Do you see patterns in your passion moments? Are you feeling more alive as you read through them? What are they telling you? Write down any thoughts you have about this first process.

When you feel ready, take out the second notebook and do the same thing. What impressions jump out at you? Are there any categories that have a consistent theme? How does your body feel when you read these highlights as a whole?

After finishing these illuminating exercises, you may feel challenged about the next steps in your life. However, you have already made a major shift in your thinking and how you view the next path on your journey. You've mindfully explored and discovered what excites you, what gives meaning to your life. And you have uncovered areas in which you can disengage, habits that don't serve you well any more.

Until more foundational work is examined, there is no easy answer to your question. Before one can jump to a conclusion of *how* to accomplish what really matters, it is necessary to dissect what is keeping you endlessly running in circles.

The answer is there, waiting for you, hidden in some deep pocket of knowledge you may be resisting. (By the way, if your results are challenging and feel too big to handle alone, make sure you get help from a counselor or coach. We do not have to take this journey alone.)

Starting with practical deeds, such as the simplicity of just acknowledging where you are right now, will take you to the next step and the next. When clarity breaks through, you will begin making decisions for yourself that matter in a more heartful way. What is your heart and mind saying? What are you doing by rote because you haven't dared to look deeper? Are you listening to your intuition—that guiding gut feeling that we so often tend to ignore?

It's all a choice. We can choose to explore our deeper nature in order to be more awake, or to make change in our families - communities and globally. Or we can stay stuck in habitual patterns that deflect our true purpose in life.

As for **awakening**, one of my favorite authors, John O'Donohue, in his book **Eternal Echoes**, explains this far better than I could. "The sacred duty of being an individual is to gradually learn to live so as to awaken the eternal within oneself…If you listen to the voices of your own longing, they will constantly call you to new styles of belonging which are energetic and mirror the complexity of your life as you deepen and intensify your presence on earth."

Dear Readers,

> Over the last few months, I have received many e.mails and telephone calls from discouraged people. And their messages all revolve around the economic situations that we are currently faced with.

One woman from Massachusetts who is undergoing chemotherapy, and running out of insurance benefits, wants help in finding a part time job that she can do from home; a senior executive from New Jersey who has been downsized is feeling frantic about earning money to help with her parent's care. I've even heard from an 80 year old man from Colorado who is worried that his $11 an hour caregiving salary is not enough to pay rent or buy food.

How I wish I could wave my magic wand and make the world a better place!

So…despite my cracked crystal ball and my slightly bent wand, I've decided to add a spiritual dimension to this column, because we need many forms of inspiration now, in addition to practical solutions.

Especially during times of challenge, we need to rely on our faith and the spiritual path that has helped us successfully journey to this particular place in time.

I realize that, in our pain and suffering, we can feel so hollow that our actions become paralyzed; and ironically, this is when we are called to greatness, to bring action and practicality center stage.

Suffering is here to teach us something. While it is present, there is also a gift for us to discover. And, while we are learning whatever it is we need to, simultaneously, this is no time to mope. (Although I give you permission for a brief one minute daily "moping" before you spring into action.)

I've discovered through the decades that every dark time I experienced invited me to reach deeper, to delve into uncharted waters that frequently seemed fearful to me. And I guarantee that **every** episode (and I had a lot of them in my younger life) resulted in astoundingly positive life changes. Had I not been given a seemingly impossible universal challenge, I would have continued to live in the anxiety and isolation of the situations as they arose and **never** would have enjoyed my many successes.

Now, I am inviting **you** to find that place of energy - your own swirling cauldron of love, mystery, challenge, fear, faith and spirit. Faith may present itself to you in various formats, but there is no doubt that each of us has a capacity for great magnitude that calls to us periodically.

Besides relying greatly on our own internal belief systems, and in responding to the appeals made to me, what **are** some questions to ask ourselves…and some practical steps we can take while we walk through uncertain times?

Let's jump right into your present situation.

1. What is your specific role in the current circumstance? For instance, do you need to make decisions for yourself, or others also?
2. Are you willing to stretch beyond (what you **think** are) present limitations?
3. Have you sought outside help? (community services, counseling, coaching, friends, family)
4. Are you committed to doing what is necessary to attain your immediate, or long term, goal?

Often, our first **reaction** to something unpleasant is to panic, and when that becomes tiring, we get to "now what?"

So…back to my questions - and, some corresponding suggestions.

1. Write, draw or scribble what your situation looks like, kind of like mind mapping. You will be surprised at what your hand hears from your brain and how it translates the messages. Using this method will give you some unexpected gifts of clarity to further reason with.

2. Millions of us at this juncture in U.S. history are called upon to think way outside the box. In order to create the best resolution, you may have to consider moving (or moving in with someone) or taking a job that you have previously believed is way outside your experience or skillset. Maybe you'll need to take some new classes, beef up your resume, scale down, temporarily take a job that you feel is beneath you. Courage and humbleness have helped many people to become great architects of their lives.

3. When times are feeling tough, we often tend to isolate, to burrow into our private world. This is when we especially need to reach out. Call your local city offices and get a list of agencies who can help you with their services. Tell your friends and family that you need advice. Get coaching or counseling for support and make a plan of action. Go to funny movies. Walk, hike, sing, swim, do yoga - get your body into action. When you're concentrating on moving your body or listening to tunes in your head, you don't have time to dwell on the stresses in your life.

4. Commitment. There is no way to substitute anything for the good old imperative of a solemn pledge to yourself. It is easy to get bogged down if too much comes at you suddenly. However, I do believe in the old saying,

slow and steady wins the race. When you create a plan, break it down into daily and weekly bite-size pieces that are doable. If remaining committed to your plan is a challenge, make yourself accountable to someone. Ask a friend to share weekly accountability sessions with you. Know that daily persistence will lead to your goal. It always does.

We have many gifts, and it's possible that we're not acknowledging them all right now. Listen to the call of your heart, to see which doors are being opened to you. Pair the opportunities with what's possible.

Shower yourself and others with gratitude and know that you will always be taken care of. How else could we have reached this day in our lives? Sometimes we simply forget the power of our own visions and the ability to manifest. You have all the answers to life's questions and challenges within your own brilliance. Allow that brilliant light to guide you to the perfect solutions. And, ummm…remember all those helpers you can call on. You are never alone.

Dear Coach Sharon,

> *My friend and I put everything we owned into a business four years ago and were just starting to succeed when the world fell apart. We borrowed heavily to start the business and used an inheritance to invest in land for our dream organization. We also bought two rental houses and thought we could turn them around for some big money. The renters have moved, we don't have the money to pay the mortgages and the bank is threatening foreclosure. We're behind on repaying*

all loans; and our business in general has plummeted. We're only 29 and 31 years old, overwhelmed, and know we've made some bad mistakes. What to do? We feel like such failures. Broke in Minnesota

Dear Minnesota Entrepreneurs,

First of all, don't beat yourselves up over this seeming catastrophe. I don't know if you are aware, but entrepreneurial-type people often go through four or five businesses until they find the *right* one. Entrepreneurs love challenges. The thrill of starting up really grooves us.

After resigning from federal government service (feds do not like entrepreneurs making their own decisions) my husband and I started a record label in 1984. Richard and I thought we had all the answers: a new idea, a gap in a huge market where we would be the pioneers, low startup costs, ingenious marketing plans, great stamina, the willingness to work hard and the intention to operate a socially conscious business...long before that term had made its appearance. At the beginning, we hired an expert consultant from the gift industry. She told us that, even though we had a *cute* idea, we would never do more than $60,000 a year. Later, with five million dollars annually in sales, we frequently laughed about almost believing her and giving up before we barely got started. But it wasn't easy. And this next paragraph may be the most important tip for you.

What we didn't know, in our entrepreneurial ignorance, was how to manage cash flow and expansion five years into the future. We got caught up in the excitement of working with big-name wholesale buyers, didn't get early financial management advice, and generally, operated by the seat of our pants…until…#5 year approached when we looked at our statements and said "what's happening?!"

Fortunately, the market we sold into was still very strong, and we were able to take evasive action immediately. It was painful taking responsibility for some of our actions, but it wasn't the end of the world.

You are young and you have not failed, but you have learned valuable lessons for your next startup. There's only the truth of what is - **the present situation**. When you can acknowledge the honesty of the circumstances (without blame) then a strong plan of action can be developed.

As you move forward, these questions and thoughts might be useful:

1. Have you gone to a strong business accountant, one who has had numerous experiences with entrepreneurial businesses? Ask this person to be upfront with you about your current position – no holding back.
2. Do you understand how courageous you were to start your businesses in the first place? Maybe it's true that you expanded a little too quickly without a solid business plan, but what did you learn from this? Make a list on paper. Do not keep it in your head. Be clear about what contributed to the demise, and successes, of your business.
3. Is there a strong vision in place for the dream you have? I work with individuals and companies all the time to help them envision the ultimate business, or life, and then create a strategic plan of action to bring the ideas to fruition. Get clear and focused.

4. Are you honest about what is really important to you…the values that stir your grits? Perhaps you've thought about what will make the most money, or will be the most exciting. However, maybe your internal consciousness is guiding you to create a business that will help millions of people to be more healthy or happy. How will you reach deep inside to discover **your** truth?

5. Have you been realistic about what is necessary to balance your life? What actions do you take to nurture yourself? Were you working 24/7 and forgot the word **burnout?** How might you begin another venture with renewed energy?

You do have some big decisions to make, and whatever they are will be perfect for you. This is an opportunity to rejuvenate yourself, acknowledge your strengths and your not-so-strengths, find professional partners that complement **your** skills…and, most importantly, create clarity about your desired outcomes and how you will achieve them.

These circumstances have presented themselves for a good reason. Be grateful and rejoice in the lessons you are learning, and know that each one has been necessary for your forward momentum.

When you were a youngster, do you remember your parents or a sports coach telling you that how you played the game was **more important than winning?** If you played **your** game with honesty, and a heartful intention to make this a better life for everyone you touched…then you have succeeded beyond all material realms.

Regroup, use your experiences to rekindle a strong foundation doing what you love, and create a better world for all of us to live in…while…incidentally making all the money that you really need, not necessarily the pile that you **want**.

Dear Coach Sharon,

I don't seem to have trouble beginning anything, but it takes so long for me to see results, that I get bored and often don't complete plans that I began with excitement and energy. Is there a magic bullet for completing projects? Frustrated in South Dakota

Dear Frustrated,

We are all different personality types. Some of us like beginnings, others like completing all the details, and some of us are so goal-oriented that we will stay with anything just to get the darn thing completed.

Many of us start businesses because we love what we do, but then the details of running a business raise their ugly head. For instance, I loved the challenge of a start-up record label, but I hated spending time with the accounting and other administrative details. As finances improved, we could hire people to take care of these things.

If my Yankee background had not prevailed, until we could get help, there might have been no pioneering development of playing and selling music in the gift industry. There is nothing wrong with any of us. We simply have different styles, and they are all perfect.

However, you do bring up an interesting idea: **Persistence As A Goal**. If you feel especially spirited with an idea and want to bask in its successful completion, what about making your goal one of perseverance?

How many of us, in our minds, have envisioned our absolute end-goal, the finale of our impassioned work? (Of course, there is *always* another goal after this.) However, what I hear often is "Sure, I know what I want, but I don't know how to get there. It takes too long. I lose energy."

In an article of *The Intelligent Optimist* magazine, the writer of a feature story about persistence, Jeremy Mercer, states … "how persistence – the ability to stay focused on goals despite obstacles and diversity – makes us who we are." I couldn't agree more. I've been proselytizing these very thoughts for decades because tenacity and dedication have resulted in my own successes through the years. **And I have often wanted to just give up**. But when I continued to follow through with one small goal, and then another and another, I was super successful.

Psychologists are defining a new trait as they re-evaluate the human personality system, and that is **persistence**. What does this word mean to you? Perhaps you only need a little assistance in how you perceive accomplishing the goal. For instance, if you have a goal of writing your own book, you might be saying to yourself, "I am writing a fascinating book and I don't know when it will be finished." Or, " I can see myself standing in my store, happy that so many people are buying my products."

Using **persistence as a goal,** you could translate this to a plan of action. "I want to complete my book by

October 30, 2017. I will write 1,000 words each day, Monday through Friday." Make it as detailed as you wish. You can imagine how committing to **this** goal will have a very different outcome.

Or, how about "I want to be promoted to head of my department sometime in the next two years. I wish my supervisor would listen to my suggestions." Does this sound wishy-washy to you?

How about making a slight transition to get where you want to be: "Every Monday morning I will write to my manager with a brief outline of my goals for the week. I will let her know that I will ask for support or clarification. At week's end, I will bullet point the highlights of the results and email them to her."

As you approach your overall goal with a plan and persist with it week after week, you have the greatest opportunity to reach exactly what you desire. This week, try your own experiment.

> Write your goal clearly.

> Make a simple plan of action for the steps you will take, for the week and month.

> Post this plan of action where you will see it all the time.

> Stay on target, one day at a time.

At the end of the week, were you closer to your weekly goal? Did you give in to distractions?

The following is a perfect persistence example that I have experienced while creating this book.

Since I've processed **Vision Mapping Strategies** with many hundreds of people, I thought it would be easy to write an book. **What the heck**, I said to myself. How difficult can it be? I soon discovered some of my own limitations.

After writing an outline of what I wanted to say, I began writing a draft. Then came the second and the third and the fourth drafts. I just wasn't happy with my results. I finally gave in and asked an editor to look over the last draft. She moved things here and there, and voila. It made sense.

Then, life and work got quite busy, and it stayed in draft form for weeks, which turned into a few months. I had lost sight of my goal, which wasn't necessarily to write a book, but to document the process for thousands of others to use, to help them move forward on their own paths to success.

I finally returned to reread what was on the printed page. All the self doubts kicked in – why would anyone want to read this, it's too short, it's too long, will readers get the full value of this process, will readers think it's stupid? Honestly now, how many of you have had similar thoughts?

So I waffled and let it sit for another few weeks, apparently fearful that the book wouldn't be successful. I know that many people don't bring their dreams to fruition because they are afraid of failure. (If any of this applies to you, please raise your hand.)

My point is that persistence, my resolve to get this published, has finally paid off. Of course, I will get an amount of money for each person who buys the book.

However, my main goal has been to navigate this process into broader environments, to support others to reach the success they dream about. Yes, it did take me a lot longer than I imagined to make this happen. But believe me…when I clicked 'publish' on the Amazon Kindle page, the feeling of accomplishment far outweighed all other emotions.

Please drop me a line and share your successes with me and the journey you took along the way. Perhaps your stories will become part of a new book. Presently, I am working on a book designed to connect heart and mind as you navigate the exploration of your life's sacred footprints.

Acknowledgements

This book has been in my head ever since I created the process of Vision Mapping Strategies in 2001. I would need pages to list all the journeyers who have blessed my path and made this possible.

Many thanks to my writing group for their continued inspirations and expertise:
>Michael Coyne
>Karen Ely
>Libbie Hawker
>Richard Hooper
>Laura Lee
>Kim Miller
>Deborah Neff
>Paul Robear
>Elinor Stutz
>Bill Weissinger

Special thanks go to Bill Weissinger, who came up with the name for this book; to Richard Hooper, who continues to inspire and motivate my writing; and, also to Libbie Hawker who taught our writing group everything we needed to know about eBooks.

If you want to know more about starting your own book writing club, please contact: Sharon@VisionJourneys.com or look up www.sharonhooper.com

Please feel free to write a review.

If you have any questions or thoughts, please email me. I want to ensure that this course is a valuable tool on your journey.
I am always open to suggestions.

Thank you to my family and friends who always support me to live a life of passion.

Thank you for purchasing this book. My reward in life is your success. If you would like to share your story with me, you know where to find me!

This program might have been easy, or challenging, for you to follow.

Dreams, goals and successful strategies take time to manifest. Great patience and perseverance may be required on your part. The most important theme resulting from these chapters might be to:

Do Some-thing, every day, every week.

If you get stalled on a particular topic, reach out to someone who will assist you through the road-block. Surround yourself with positive people who support your objectives. Staying stuck uses valuable time that you can be using to advance your strategic plan of action.

On the other hand, if you need time to research or process thoughts, take all the time you need. This is your plan, your dream. You get to call the shots.

Create positive intention to carry through with your agenda. Successful results take place when you believe in yourself, persevere and take the necessary steps to accomplish your targeted goals and dreams.

Thank you so much for being part of my journey. You make it possible for me to live my dream, which is supporting others to be super successful in life and business.

**Passion + knowledge + clarity
+ perseverance + action =**

Resounding success

Sharon Hooper is a Professional Certified Coach with over four decades of successful business experience. After becoming president of an independent record company, she was responsible for the novel marketing strategies and sales leadership that enabled a small start-up business to become a successful multi-million dollar international company. As a coach, Sharon's passion, and creative approaches to business and life challenges, has helped hundreds of other people to reach their goals and achieve the success they have always dreamed of. Sharon lives in the NW with her author husband, Richard, and two uppity cats.

As a Professional Certified Coach Sharon is available for individual or group coaching and/or consulting--in person, via Skype or by telephone.

Made in the USA
San Bernardino, CA
15 September 2019